MY Mindfulness Matters

D1736497

Debbie Chamberlain

Helen Minor

Dedicated to our family, friends, and students who taught us how to live, laugh, and love.

MY mindfulness matters
each day,

and helps me live in a
mindful way!

I am learning to be present
in the here and now.

Follow me and I'll show you how.

Mindful Moment
What is Mindfulness?
Mindfulness is being aware of the present moment with curiosity.

BE in this moment and notice....

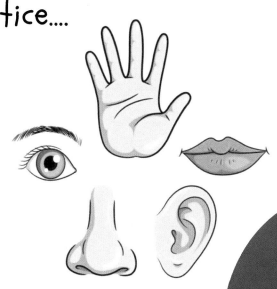

5 things you SEE

4 things you HEAR

3 things you can FEEL

2 things you can SMELL

1 thing you like to TASTE

MY feelings and emotions are all okay.

I listen to what they have to say.

Mindful Moment

Emotions

Look in a mirror and show an emotion on your face.

What does your face look like when you are.....

SAD

HAPPY

MAD

EXCITED

SURPRISED

MY breath calms my mind and peace starts to grow.

My strong emotions pause so I can let them go.

Mindful Moment
Star Breathing

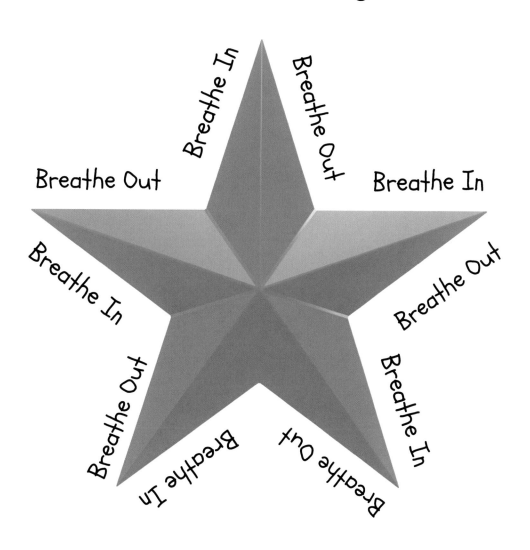

MY amazing brain knows exactly
what to do,

when I'm feeling mad,
scared, or blue.

Mindful Moment
Parts of the Brain

PreFrontal Cortex
Wise Owl

This part of your brain helps you make good decisions!

Amygdala
Guard Dog

This part of your brain feels your feelings and keeps you safe!

Hippocampus
Memory Saver

This part of your brain helps you to remember!

MY heart leads me to
love and care,

for everyone and everything,
everywhere.

Mindful Moment
Heartfulness

How do you spread heartfulness?

PLAY WITH SOMEONE NEW!

SAY HELLO!

WRITE A KIND NOTE!

PICK UP TRASH

SMILE AT SOMEONE

SAY THANK YOU!

MY mindfulness reminds me
to go slow,

to listen, to love, and let life flow.

Mindful Moment

Equanimity - calm state of mind

Emotions will come and go.......
just like a storm.

Remember that hard times
won't last forever.

MY story is unique and all my own.

I'm proud of myself and how
much I've grown.

Mindful Moment
Growth Mindset

Tell Yourself....

I can do hard things!

MY family loves and believes in me,

in all my hopes and my dreams.

MY friends are people that care,

who listen to all that I
want to share.

Mindful Moment

Connection with others

Send people you love a kind thought......

I hope you are happy.

I hope you are safe.

I hope you have a great day!

Mindful Moment
Self Love

I am Brave I am Me

I am Kind

I am Loving

What do you love about yourself?

MY mindful tools
guide me through,

my strong emotions and
thoughts too.

Mindful Moment

Mindful Toolbox

 Listen to Music

 Positive Self Talk

 Exercise

 Breathe

 Mindful Coloring

 Journal

 Forgive

 Be in Nature

And through it all,
MY mindful mind,

reminds me to be present
with a heart that's kind.

Mindful Moment

Empathy

Thinking about other people's feelings
and showing that you care.

Listen   Love   Encourage

What a wonderful
world it would be,

If we all just took a
moment to breathe.

Be the person you needed when you were younger.

Debbie and Helen spent decades teaching elementary school students and absolutely loved it!
Their vision embraces the importance of teaching children to love themselves with their whole heart and embrace all that makes them unique and special!

Words for Teachers and Caregivers

Hello and thank you for purchasing this book! We wrote this with so much love and care and hope you find it useful in your classroom or home. Many mindful tools are introduced so you may enjoy sharing this book again and again!

The "Mindful Moment" pages are there for you to participate in activities to practice mindful tools.

Mindfulness, empathy, self-love and how it all works together to create the best versions of ourselves helps create supportive, loving communities.

We titled the book MY mindfulness matters as a reminder that our wellness starts with our individual efforts to live each day in a mindful way.

What is mindfulness?

Mindfulness is paying attention to the present moment with curiosity and care.

What mindfulness is not.

Mindfulness isn't thinking about nothing or being happy all the time.

Why Mindfulness?

Improves self regulation

Reduces stress, anxiety, and depression

Increases compassion and empathy

Improves focus and concentration

Myndfulness Matters

EDUCATING • EMPOWERING

Made in the USA
Middletown, DE
21 February 2022

61307376R00018